PRINCEWILL LAGANG

Mindful Separation: Navigating Breakups Respectfully

First published by PRINCEWILL LAGANG 2023

Copyright © 2023 by Princewill Lagang

All rights reserved. No part of this publication may be reproduced, stored or transmitted in any form or by any means, electronic, mechanical, photocopying, recording, scanning, or otherwise without written permission from the publisher. It is illegal to copy this book, post it to a website, or distribute it by any other means without permission.

Princewill Lagang asserts the moral right to be identified as the author of this work.

First edition

*This book was professionally typeset on Reedsy.
Find out more at reedsy.com*

Contents

1	Introduction	1
2	The Decision to Separate	4
3	Honoring Shared History	7
4	The Role of Communication	9
5	Mutual Respect and Dignity	12
6	Navigating Emotional Turmoil	15
7	Transitioning Mindfully	18
8	Supporting Children and Families	21
9	Maintaining Boundaries	24
10	Healing and Growth	27
11	Co-Parenting After Separation	30
12	Reflection and Moving Forward	33

1

Introduction

Breakups with Mindfulness and Respect: Navigating the Path to Healing

In a world where relationships play a pivotal role in our lives, the journey of parting ways often remains an uncharted territory of emotions, uncertainties, and challenges. This book, "Breakups with Mindfulness and Respect: Navigating the Path to Healing," aims to shed light on an approach that encourages individuals to approach the difficult terrain of breakups with a heightened sense of awareness, mindfulness, and respect.

1.1 Embracing the Uncomfortable:

The dissolution of a relationship, whether a romantic partnership or a friendship, is an inevitable part of the human experience. Yet, the manner in which we navigate these endings can have a profound impact on our emotional well-being, personal growth, and future relationships. This book seeks to explore the idea that by embracing the discomfort of breakups and treating them as opportunities for growth, we can emerge from these experiences stronger, more self-aware, and better equipped to create healthier connections in the future.

1.2 The Significance of Healthy Endings:

The way we end relationships matters just as much as the way we begin them. Breakups that are marked by bitterness, resentment, and animosity can leave lasting scars on our emotional landscape, affecting our self-esteem and ability to trust. Conversely, endings that are approached with mindfulness and respect lay the foundation for mutual understanding, closure, and a healthier emotional aftermath.

1.3 Mindfulness as a Path to Healing:

Mindfulness, often associated with practices like meditation and self-awareness, is a tool that can guide us through the tumultuous waters of a breakup. By staying present with our emotions, thoughts, and reactions, we can cultivate a greater sense of clarity about our feelings, desires, and needs. Mindfulness also enables us to respond to challenges with intention and compassion rather than reacting impulsively out of pain or anger.

1.4 Navigating Respectful Communication:

Respectful communication is at the heart of approaching breakups mindfully. Learning to communicate our feelings and intentions with empathy and authenticity can foster a sense of closure and understanding. This book will delve into effective strategies for initiating conversations, expressing emotions constructively, and listening actively – all of which contribute to maintaining dignity and honor throughout the breakup process.

1.5 The Structure of the Book:

This book is divided into several chapters, each addressing a specific aspect of the breakup journey. We will explore the emotional rollercoaster that often accompanies breakups, provide insights into managing post-breakup challenges, and offer guidance on self-care and personal growth during this transformative phase. Additionally, real-life stories and practical exercises will be interspersed throughout to provide relatable examples and actionable steps.

INTRODUCTION

In the pages that follow, we will embark on a journey of self-discovery, healing, and transformation. By approaching breakups with mindfulness and respect, we can navigate the path to healing with grace and emerge from the experience as stronger and wiser individuals.

2

The Decision to Separate

2.1 The Crossroads of Emotions and Reflection:

The decision to end a relationship is a pivotal moment that often marks the intersection of complex emotions and reflective contemplation. At this juncture, individuals find themselves grappling with a myriad of feelings, ranging from doubt and sadness to relief and apprehension. This chapter delves into the process of arriving at the decision to separate, emphasizing the significance of self-awareness, introspection, and open communication.

2.2 The Power of Self-Reflection:

Before any relationship can come to an end, there exists an internal dialogue that demands attention. Self-reflection becomes a guiding light during this time, as individuals assess their emotions, values, and needs. Taking the time to introspect allows for a deeper understanding of whether the relationship aligns with one's personal growth, happiness, and well-being. By honestly acknowledging the reasons behind the decision, individuals pave the way for a more constructive and authentic separation.

2.3 Navigating Difficult Conversations:

Once the decision to separate is internalized, the next step is to share this revelation with the partner. Honesty and clarity are paramount during this process. It's essential to approach the conversation with empathy, focusing on mutual understanding rather than blame. This chapter provides practical advice on how to initiate these conversations, maintain emotional composure, and ensure that both parties have an opportunity to express their feelings and perspectives.

2.4 Recognizing Patterns and Growth Opportunities:
Often, the decision to separate comes after a period of recognizing patterns of behavior, compatibility issues, or unmet needs. This phase of reflection serves as an opportunity for growth and learning, allowing individuals to identify areas of personal development that can enrich future relationships. By acknowledging these patterns, individuals can ensure that the decision to separate is made from a place of self-respect and empowerment.

2.5 The Importance of Mutual Agreement:
In situations where both partners acknowledge the need for separation, mutual agreement can lay the foundation for a more amicable transition. Mutual respect and understanding can foster a cooperative mindset that enables both parties to work together to navigate the complexities of ending the relationship. This chapter outlines the benefits of approaching separation as a shared decision rather than a unilateral choice.

2.6 Cultivating Emotional Preparedness:
The decision to separate is often fraught with a range of emotions that can be overwhelming. This chapter provides insights into preparing emotionally for the aftermath of the decision. By acknowledging the emotions that may arise post-separation and developing strategies to cope with them, individuals can navigate the journey ahead with a sense of resilience and self-care.

In the following chapters, we will delve deeper into the practical aspects of respectful communication, emotional healing, and personal growth during and after a breakup. By recognizing the significance of the decision to separate and approaching it with mindfulness and respect, individuals can lay the groundwork for a more constructive and transformative journey.

3

Honoring Shared History

3.1 Embracing the Complexity of Memories:
When a relationship comes to an end, it's natural to focus on the reasons for the separation and the challenges that were faced. However, it's equally important to acknowledge and honor the positive aspects of the shared history. This chapter invites individuals to embrace the complexity of their memories, highlighting the moments of joy, growth, and connection that were an integral part of the relationship.

3.2 Recognizing Growth and Learning:
Every relationship, regardless of its duration, offers opportunities for personal growth and learning. By reflecting on the lessons learned, the strengths discovered, and the changes undergone, individuals can appreciate the transformative power of their time together. This chapter emphasizes the value of recognizing how the relationship contributed to the development of essential life skills and a deeper understanding of oneself.

3.3 Shifting Perspectives on Endings:
Society often portrays the end of a relationship as a failure. However, this chapter encourages a shift in perspective, inviting readers to view the end

as a transition rather than a defeat. By acknowledging that the relationship served its purpose and played a role in shaping the individuals involved, it becomes possible to see the breakup as a step toward new opportunities and personal evolution.

3.4 The Ritual of Closure:

Rituals can play a meaningful role in honoring the shared history of a relationship. Creating a ritual of closure – whether through a heartfelt conversation, a symbolic gesture, or a written letter – can provide a sense of closure and allow both individuals to express their gratitude, forgiveness, and well wishes. This chapter provides suggestions for designing personal rituals that align with the unique dynamics of the relationship.

3.5 Shared Experiences as Building Blocks:

The experiences shared within the relationship form a foundation upon which personal growth can continue to flourish. This chapter explores the concept of using these shared experiences as building blocks for the future, emphasizing the importance of integrating the positive aspects of the relationship into one's narrative while moving forward.

3.6 Navigating Nostalgia:

After a breakup, feelings of nostalgia can be bittersweet. This chapter addresses the role of nostalgia in the healing process and provides guidance on how to navigate it. By learning to appreciate the memories without clinging to them, individuals can find a healthy balance between honoring the past and embracing the present.

As we move forward in our exploration, we will delve into the intricacies of respectful communication during and after a breakup. By recognizing the value of honoring shared history, individuals can create a bridge between their past and their future, fostering a sense of closure and allowing space for new beginnings.

4

The Role of Communication

4.1 The Foundation of Respectful Breakups:
Effective communication serves as the cornerstone of approaching breakups with mindfulness and respect. It is through communication that individuals can navigate the complexities of their emotions, share their perspectives, and work towards mutual understanding. This chapter emphasizes the pivotal role of communication in the breakup process and its potential to foster a sense of dignity and closure.

4.2 Honesty as a Guiding Principle:
Openness and honesty form the bedrock of any successful breakup conversation. This chapter highlights the importance of approaching the conversation with authenticity, sharing one's feelings, concerns, and thoughts without sugar-coating or evasion. By being forthright, both individuals can engage in a dialogue that promotes clarity and minimizes misunderstandings.

4.3 Expressing Emotions with Compassion:
Breakups can be emotionally charged experiences, and expressing these feelings requires a delicate balance of vulnerability and empathy. This chapter delves into strategies for communicating emotions with compassion, such

as using "I" statements to express personal feelings and avoiding blame or accusations. By acknowledging the emotions of both parties, a safe space for open dialogue can be established.

4.4 Initiating the Conversation:

The act of initiating the breakup conversation can be daunting. This chapter offers practical guidance on how to approach this pivotal moment. It emphasizes the importance of choosing an appropriate time and setting, and provides suggestions for framing the conversation in a way that is sensitive, respectful, and focused on the shared well-being of both individuals.

4.5 Active Listening and Validation:

Effective communication involves not only expressing oneself but also actively listening to the other person's perspective. This chapter explores the art of active listening and validation, showing how these skills can contribute to a more constructive conversation. By creating a space where both individuals feel heard and understood, the potential for healing and closure is enhanced.

4.6 Finding Common Ground:

Despite the decision to separate, finding common ground can help bridge the gap between the individuals involved. This chapter discusses strategies for identifying shared goals, values, or interests that can be acknowledged and appreciated, fostering a sense of connection and closure. By focusing on what was positive in the relationship, both parties can part ways with a shared sense of respect.

4.7 The Value of Closure:

A well-communicated breakup conversation offers the gift of closure, allowing both individuals to find a sense of completion and understanding. This chapter underscores the significance of concluding the conversation in a way that leaves no loose ends, ensuring that both individuals have had the opportunity to express themselves fully and are aligned in their understanding of the decision.

As we move forward in our exploration, we will delve into the process of emotional healing after a breakup and the strategies for nurturing personal growth. By recognizing the importance of effective communication, individuals can pave the way for a healthier and more transformative journey through the complexities of separation.

5

Mutual Respect and Dignity

5.1 The Essence of Respectful Separation:

In the midst of the emotional whirlwind that accompanies breakups, it's essential to anchor the process in mutual respect and dignity. This chapter underscores the importance of treating each other with kindness, empathy, and consideration, regardless of the challenges being faced. By upholding these principles, both individuals can navigate the breakup journey with integrity and grace.

5.2 Treating Each Other as Equals:

The dynamics of a breakup can sometimes lead to power imbalances or attempts to assign blame. This chapter emphasizes the value of treating each other as equals, recognizing that both individuals are entitled to their feelings, perspectives, and experiences. Approaching the separation as a collaborative process, rather than a contest, fosters an atmosphere of respect and shared responsibility.

5.3 Kindness Even in Disagreement:

Difficult conversations during a breakup can be emotionally charged and prone to friction. However, this chapter explores the transformative power of maintaining kindness and empathy even in the face of disagreements. By acknowledging that both individuals are navigating their emotions, it becomes possible to foster a sense of compassion that can temper the intensity of the conversation.

5.4 Focusing on Behaviors, Not Personal Attacks:
Disagreements and conflicts may arise during a breakup, but it's crucial to focus on addressing specific behaviors rather than resorting to personal attacks. This chapter provides strategies for communicating boundaries, expressing concerns, and discussing issues while avoiding hurtful language. By directing the conversation toward behavior rather than character, respect remains intact.

5.5 Finding Common Ground in the Midst of Differences:
Even in the process of separation, there are often areas of agreement and shared values that can be recognized. This chapter explores the significance of identifying common ground and using it as a foundation for productive conversations. By building upon shared understanding, both individuals can work towards a more amicable and respectful resolution.

5.6 Embracing the Power of Empathy:
Empathy allows individuals to step into each other's shoes and understand the emotional landscape of the other person. This chapter delves into the role of empathy in promoting mutual respect and dignity during a breakup. By acknowledging each other's feelings and perspectives, both parties can create an environment that fosters understanding rather than animosity.

5.7 Closure Through Mutual Respect:
The chapter concludes by emphasizing that the journey of a respectful breakup is not just about the end of a relationship but also about the beginning of a new phase marked by personal growth. By treating each other with respect and dignity, both individuals can find closure that paves the way for healing, transformation, and the possibility of healthy future connections.

As we progress in our exploration, we will delve into the process of emotional healing and the strategies for nurturing personal growth after a breakup. By recognizing the profound impact of mutual respect and dignity, individuals can navigate the complexities of separation while maintaining their integrity and grace.

6

Navigating Emotional Turmoil

6.1 The Emotional Landscape of Breakups:

Breakups often lead to a rollercoaster of emotions, ranging from grief and sadness to anger and confusion. This chapter acknowledges the emotional challenges that individuals face during this turbulent phase and emphasizes the importance of navigating these feelings with self-compassion and resilience.

6.2 Allowing Space for Grief:

Grief is a natural response to the loss of a relationship. This chapter explores the stages of grief and provides insights into how individuals can allow themselves to experience and process these emotions. By acknowledging and validating their feelings of loss, individuals can create a space for healing and emotional growth.

6.3 Practicing Emotional Awareness:

Mindfulness of emotions is a crucial tool for managing emotional turmoil during a breakup. This chapter discusses the practice of emotional awareness, which involves observing and labeling one's emotions without judgment. By becoming attuned to their emotional states, individuals can respond to their feelings with greater clarity and self-understanding.

6.4 Techniques for Managing Anger and Resentment:
Anger and resentment can be common emotions during a breakup, often stemming from unmet expectations or feelings of betrayal. This chapter offers techniques for managing these intense emotions, including deep breathing exercises, journaling, and practicing forgiveness. By addressing anger constructively, individuals can prevent it from escalating into harmful behaviors.

6.5 Finding Solace in Self-Care:
Self-care plays a pivotal role in navigating emotional turmoil. This chapter emphasizes the value of engaging in activities that promote physical, mental, and emotional well-being. From exercise and meditation to creative pursuits and spending time with loved ones, self-care provides a means of coping and finding solace amidst the storm of emotions.

6.6 Seeking Support from Loved Ones:
During a breakup, the support of friends and family can provide a vital lifeline. This chapter explores the importance of reaching out for emotional support, discussing feelings with trusted confidantes, and allowing oneself to lean on others during difficult times. Connection and shared experiences can offer comfort and a sense of belonging.

6.7 Professional Help and Counseling:
In some cases, the emotional turmoil of a breakup may necessitate professional support. This chapter discusses the benefits of seeking counseling or therapy to navigate complex emotions and develop coping strategies. Professional guidance can offer valuable insights and tools for processing feelings and moving forward with resilience.

6.8 The Path to Healing:
The chapter concludes by highlighting that the journey of emotional

turmoil is not one of avoidance but of navigation. By practicing emotional awareness, self-compassion, and seeking support when needed, individuals can progress along the path to healing. The emotional landscape of a breakup can be transformative, leading to personal growth and greater self-awareness.

In the upcoming chapters, we will delve into the process of personal growth and transformation after a breakup. By acknowledging and managing the emotional challenges with mindfulness and self-care, individuals can pave the way for a healthier and more resilient future.

7

Transitioning Mindfully

7.1 The Practical Side of Moving On:

As a breakup unfolds, there are practical considerations that need attention, particularly when transitioning out of a shared living situation. This chapter addresses the logistics of separating physical spaces and belongings, emphasizing the importance of approaching these tasks mindfully and respectfully.

7.2 Establishing Clear Boundaries:

Clear boundaries are crucial during the process of transitioning out of a shared living situation. This chapter discusses the importance of establishing boundaries related to living arrangements, personal space, and communication. By setting these boundaries, individuals can minimize misunderstandings and create a more harmonious transition.

7.3 Communication and Planning:

Effective communication and planning are key to a smooth transition. This chapter delves into strategies for discussing logistics, such as moving timelines, distribution of belongings, and financial responsibilities. Open and respectful conversations can lead to practical solutions that prioritize both individuals' needs.

7.4 Dividing Belongings:

The division of shared belongings can be emotionally charged. This chapter provides guidance on how to approach this process with sensitivity and fairness. By creating an inventory of possessions, openly discussing preferences, and focusing on equitable distribution, individuals can navigate this aspect of the transition more smoothly.

7.5 Finding New Living Arrangements:

In cases where one or both individuals need to find new living arrangements, the process can be both challenging and transformative. This chapter discusses considerations for finding new homes, whether it's renting a place, moving in with friends or family, or seeking shared housing. It also encourages individuals to approach this change as an opportunity for personal growth.

7.6 Transitioning Children and Pets:

If children or pets are involved, their well-being must be prioritized during the transition. This chapter addresses the importance of maintaining stability for them and working out a plan that ensures their needs are met. Cooperation and open communication between both individuals are essential to create a nurturing environment for everyone involved.

7.7 Navigating Legal and Financial Matters:

Legal and financial matters may arise during a breakup, particularly if individuals shared assets or financial responsibilities. This chapter offers insights into approaching these matters mindfully and responsibly. Seeking legal advice and ensuring fairness can help prevent future conflicts and facilitate a smoother transition.

7.8 Embracing Change and Transformation:

The transition out of a shared living situation signifies the start of a new chapter. This chapter concludes by emphasizing the importance of embracing change and transformation. By viewing this period as an opportunity for personal growth, individuals can approach the future with a sense of resilience and optimism.

In the upcoming chapters, we will delve into the process of personal growth and transformation after a breakup, and strategies for creating a positive and fulfilling post-breakup life. By addressing the practical aspects of transitioning mindfully, individuals can pave the way for a smoother and more respectful journey toward new beginnings.

8

Supporting Children and Families

8.1 Ripple Effects of a Breakup:
A breakup has a far-reaching impact that extends beyond the individuals directly involved. This chapter delves into the complexities of how children and extended family members are affected by the separation. It emphasizes the importance of approaching these relationships with sensitivity, open communication, and a shared commitment to the well-being of all parties involved.

8.2 Understanding Children's Perspectives:
Children often experience a mix of emotions when their parents or guardians go through a breakup. This chapter discusses the range of feelings that children may have, including confusion, sadness, anger, and even guilt. By recognizing and validating these emotions, adults can create a supportive environment that helps children navigate the changes more effectively.

8.3 Maintaining Consistency and Routine:
During a breakup, maintaining consistency and routine can provide children with a sense of stability. This chapter explores strategies for ensuring that daily routines and familiar activities are upheld as much as possible.

Consistency can help children feel secure in a time of change and uncertainty.

8.4 Co-Parenting with Respect:

Co-parenting requires effective communication, cooperation, and mutual respect. This chapter discusses the importance of co-parenting with sensitivity to the needs of the children. It provides insights into creating a co-parenting plan that addresses custody arrangements, decision-making, and ongoing communication to ensure the children's well-being remains a top priority.

8.5 Navigating Extended Family Dynamics:

A breakup can impact relationships with extended family members, such as in-laws and mutual friends. This chapter addresses the complexities of these relationships and provides strategies for maintaining boundaries, addressing potential conflicts, and nurturing connections that are valuable to all parties involved.

8.6 Encouraging Open Dialogue:

Open dialogue is essential in supporting children and extended family members during a breakup. This chapter offers guidance on fostering open conversations with children about the changes and ensuring they feel heard and understood. It also suggests ways to address questions and concerns from extended family members with empathy and respect.

8.7 Professional Support for Children:

In some cases, children may benefit from professional support, such as counseling or therapy, to help them navigate the emotional challenges of a breakup. This chapter discusses the role of professional help in providing children with a safe space to express their feelings and develop coping strategies.

8.8 Honoring Bonds and Shared Memories:

The chapter concludes by emphasizing the importance of honoring the bonds and shared memories that exist within the extended family. By nurturing these connections, individuals can create a supportive network that contributes to the emotional well-being of everyone involved.

In the upcoming chapters, we will delve into the process of personal growth and transformation after a breakup, and strategies for creating a positive and fulfilling post-breakup life. By recognizing and addressing the impact on children and extended family members, individuals can navigate the complexities of shared relationships with empathy and understanding.

9

Maintaining Boundaries

9.1 The Role of Boundaries in Post-Breakup Life:

Boundaries serve as essential guideposts in maintaining healthy post-breakup dynamics. This chapter delves into the significance of setting and respecting boundaries as individuals navigate the complexities of separation and transformation. By establishing clear boundaries, individuals can promote emotional well-being and facilitate smoother interactions.

9.2 Setting Emotional Boundaries:

Emotional boundaries are crucial for safeguarding one's mental and emotional health. This chapter discusses the importance of defining personal emotional limits and communicating them effectively. By identifying what types of interactions are comfortable and respectful, individuals can avoid unnecessary emotional turmoil.

9.3 Practicing Physical Boundaries:

Physical boundaries encompass personal space and touch. This chapter explores the significance of practicing physical boundaries to ensure comfort and respect. It provides insights into communicating physical boundaries with empathy and addressing situations where physical proximity might pose challenges.

9.4 Navigating Communication Boundaries:

Communication boundaries play a pivotal role in post-breakup interactions. This chapter discusses strategies for maintaining effective communication without overstepping boundaries. By setting expectations for frequency, modes of communication, and topics of discussion, individuals can avoid misunderstandings and potential conflicts.

9.5 Respecting Shared Spaces:

When individuals continue to share spaces, such as workplaces or social circles, it's essential to set boundaries that respect each other's presence. This chapter explores approaches to navigating shared spaces, emphasizing the importance of courteous behavior, maintaining professionalism, and minimizing potential discomfort.

9.6 Coexisting on Social Media:

In the digital age, social media can complicate post-breakup dynamics. This chapter provides insights into establishing boundaries on social media platforms, such as adjusting privacy settings and deciding whether to maintain online connections. By navigating these spaces mindfully, individuals can prevent unnecessary emotional distress.

9.7 Adjusting Friendships and Mutual Contacts:

Shared friendships and mutual contacts can present challenges after a breakup. This chapter discusses the importance of respecting each other's relationships and considering whether adjustments are needed in shared social circles. By communicating openly and focusing on respectful coexistence, individuals can navigate these dynamics with grace.

9.8 Supporting Boundaries with Self-Care:

The chapter concludes by highlighting the synergy between boundaries and self-care. By setting and maintaining boundaries, individuals can create the space needed for self-care routines that promote emotional well-being. In turn, self-care reinforces the ability to uphold boundaries effectively.

In the upcoming chapters, we will delve into the process of personal growth and transformation after a breakup, and strategies for creating a positive and fulfilling post-breakup life. By recognizing the importance of boundaries and practicing respectful communication and interactions, individuals can navigate the complexities of post-breakup relationships with integrity and empowerment.

10

Healing and Growth

10.1 Embracing the Journey of Healing:
After the storm of a breakup, the journey of healing and personal growth begins. This chapter delves into the phases of healing, emphasizing the importance of allowing oneself to grieve, reflect, and eventually embark on a transformative path towards self-discovery and empowerment.

10.2 Nurturing Self-Compassion:
Self-compassion is a fundamental component of healing after a breakup. This chapter discusses the importance of treating oneself with kindness and understanding. By practicing self-compassion, individuals can navigate the emotional challenges of healing with greater resilience and self-awareness.

10.3 Allowing Time for Reflection:
Reflection is a powerful tool for self-discovery and growth. This chapter explores the process of reflecting on the relationship, the breakup, and the lessons learned. By allowing time for introspection, individuals can gain insights into their desires, needs, and the patterns that shape their relationships.

10.4 Practicing Forgiveness:

Forgiveness, both for oneself and for the other person, is a transformative aspect of healing. This chapter discusses the role of forgiveness in releasing emotional burdens and fostering personal growth. By letting go of resentment and embracing forgiveness, individuals can free themselves from the weight of the past.

10.5 Cultivating New Interests and Passions:

Post-breakup is a time for rediscovering oneself. This chapter explores the value of exploring new interests, hobbies, and passions as a means of self-expression and personal growth. Engaging in activities that bring joy and fulfillment can contribute to building a positive post-breakup life.

10.6 Creating a Supportive Network:

Building a network of supportive relationships is essential for healing and growth. This chapter discusses the role of friends, family, and possibly therapy or counseling in providing emotional support. By nurturing these connections, individuals can feel less isolated and more empowered in their journey.

10.7 Setting New Goals and Intentions:

Setting new goals and intentions is a powerful way to channel post-breakup energy. This chapter emphasizes the significance of establishing personal goals, whether they're related to career, personal development, or relationships. By focusing on growth, individuals can create a sense of purpose and direction.

10.8 Finding Closure and Moving Forward:

Closure is not a single event but a gradual process that involves finding peace with the past. This chapter discusses strategies for achieving closure, such as writing a letter to the former partner, participating in symbolic rituals, and embracing the changes that come with moving forward.

10.9 Embracing a Positive Post-Breakup Life:

The chapter concludes by emphasizing that healing and growth are ongoing processes that lead to a positive post-breakup life. By acknowledging the strength gained from navigating the challenges of separation, individuals can approach the future with a renewed sense of self-worth, resilience, and possibility.

In the final chapter of our exploration, we will reflect on the transformative journey of approaching breakups with mindfulness and respect. By embracing healing and growth, individuals can emerge from the experience with greater self-awareness and the ability to cultivate healthier relationships moving forward.

11

Co-Parenting After Separation

11.1 The Journey of Co-Parenting:

Co-parenting after a breakup is a unique journey that presents both challenges and opportunities for personal growth. This chapter delves into the complexities of co-parenting, emphasizing the importance of maintaining a child-centered approach and effective communication.

11.2 Navigating Co-Parenting Challenges:

Co-parenting can bring about various challenges, including differences in parenting styles, communication issues, and emotional dynamics. This chapter discusses strategies for addressing these challenges and maintaining a cooperative co-parenting relationship that prioritizes the well-being of the children involved.

11.3 Fostering Effective Communication:

Effective communication is the cornerstone of successful co-parenting. This chapter explores strategies for maintaining open lines of communication, whether through in-person conversations, phone calls, emails, or messaging apps. By focusing on clear, respectful, and child-centered communication, co-parents can work together more harmoniously.

11.4 Shared Responsibilities and Decision-Making:

Co-parenting involves shared responsibilities and joint decision-making. This chapter discusses how co-parents can navigate decisions related to the children's education, healthcare, extracurricular activities, and more. It emphasizes the importance of involving both parents in the decision-making process to create a sense of partnership.

11.5 Creating a Parenting Plan:

A well-structured parenting plan is a crucial tool for co-parenting. This chapter provides insights into developing a comprehensive parenting plan that outlines custody arrangements, visitation schedules, and other practical details. By having a clear plan in place, co-parents can reduce ambiguity and potential conflicts.

11.6 Managing Transitions and Visitation:

Transitioning between co-parenting households can be challenging for children. This chapter discusses strategies for managing transitions smoothly, creating a sense of consistency, and minimizing stress for the children. By focusing on their comfort and well-being, co-parents can facilitate a positive adjustment.

11.7 Keeping Children Out of Conflict:

Shielding children from parental conflicts is paramount. This chapter explores the importance of maintaining a respectful and cooperative tone, both in front of the children and in private conversations. By prioritizing the children's emotional well-being, co-parents can create a stable environment.

11.8 Embracing the Benefits of Co-Parenting:

Co-parenting offers numerous benefits for both the children and the parents. This chapter discusses the positive impact of continued involvement from both parents, including increased emotional support, diverse perspectives, and shared responsibilities. By embracing these benefits, co-parents can foster a nurturing and balanced environment.

11.9 Seeking Professional Support:

In some cases, professional support, such as family counseling or mediation, may be beneficial for co-parents. This chapter discusses how seeking outside help can facilitate effective communication, conflict resolution, and the development of a successful co-parenting dynamic.

11.10 Empowering Children Through Co-Parenting:

The chapter concludes by emphasizing that co-parenting is an opportunity to model respectful relationships and empower children with valuable life skills. By approaching co-parenting with empathy, communication, and a shared commitment to the children's well-being, individuals can contribute to their children's growth and development.

As we come to the end of our exploration, we reflect on the transformative journey of approaching breakups with mindfulness and respect. By embracing the challenges and opportunities of co-parenting, individuals can create a positive and nurturing environment for themselves and their children, fostering growth, resilience, and mutual understanding.

12

Reflection and Moving Forward

12.1 Embracing the Journey of Mindful Separation:
The journey of mindful separation has been one of self-discovery, growth, and transformation. This final chapter invites you to reflect on the lessons learned, the challenges overcome, and the progress made in approaching breakups with mindfulness and respect.

12.2 Lessons Learned and Personal Growth:
Mindful separation has taught you that endings can also be beginnings. This chapter discusses the lessons you've gained from navigating the complexities of separation, including the importance of open communication, setting boundaries, and nurturing self-compassion. These lessons have contributed to your personal growth and resilience.

12.3 The Power of Self-Reflection:
Reflecting on your journey allows you to see the evolution of your emotional landscape. This chapter encourages you to revisit your thoughts, emotions, and actions throughout the process. By acknowledging your progress and celebrating your achievements, you can reinforce a sense of empowerment and self-awareness.

12.4 Cultivating Mindfulness and Respect:

The journey of mindful separation has highlighted the profound impact of approaching breakups with mindfulness and respect. This chapter summarizes the key principles of respectful communication, emotional healing, setting boundaries, and co-parenting. These principles serve as a foundation for healthier relationships in the future.

12.5 Fostering Positive Future Connections:

Moving forward, the journey of mindful separation equips you with tools for building healthier and more fulfilling relationships. This chapter discusses the importance of carrying forward the lessons learned, practicing self-awareness, and approaching future connections with the wisdom gained from your experience.

12.6 Celebrating New Beginnings:

The chapter concludes by emphasizing that mindful separation marks not just an end but a new beginning. By embracing the changes, growth, and resilience that have emerged from the journey, you can step into the future with a sense of empowerment and optimism. Each new chapter holds the potential for growth and positive transformation.

As you close this chapter and embark on your post-breakup life, remember that the journey of mindful separation has equipped you with the tools to create a positive and fulfilling future. By applying the principles of mindful communication, self-compassion, and respectful interactions, you can approach relationships with a sense of intention and empowerment. Thank you for joining us on this transformative journey.

www.ingramcontent.com/pod-product-compliance
Lightning Source LLC
LaVergne TN
LVHW010441070526
838199LV00066B/6126